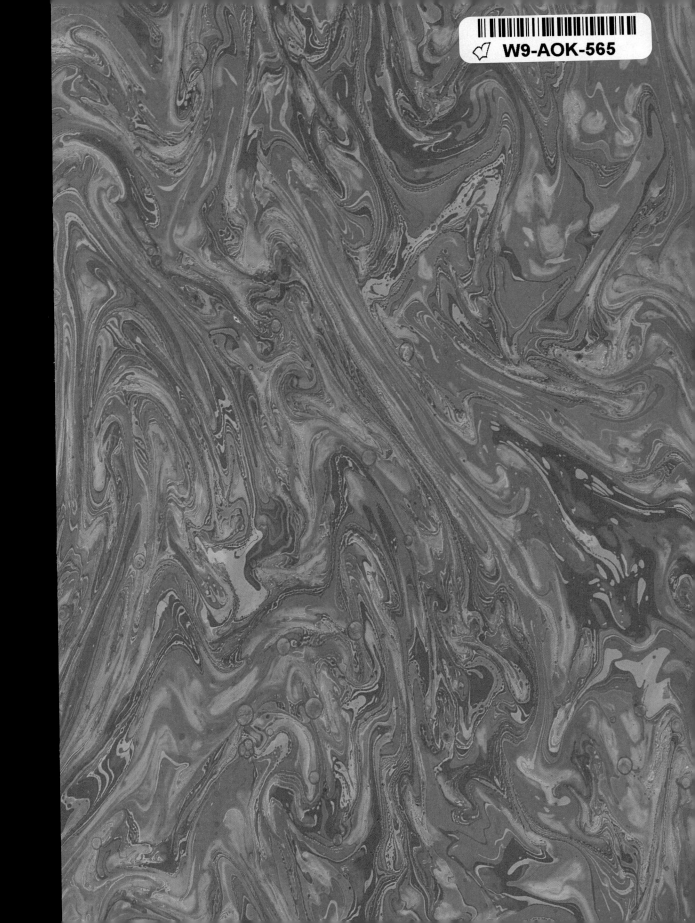

CLOSE TO HOME

CLOSE TO HOME

— A Canadian Country Diary —

STEWART HOUSE
BOULTON PUBLISHING

THIS BOOK is dedicated to my wife Patti
and to the memory of her father
Charles David Copeland.

Special thanks are due to the following people for their
support and encouragement: Roger Boulton,
Catherine Craig, Janis Duffy, Ray Francisco, Elene Freer,
Pat and Madge Montgomery, Bert and Patty Naylor,
Dr. Jonathon Schmidt, Rev. Kim and Wilma Warne,
George and Barbara Wilson; also my parents
Jack and Lois Ivy.

Produced by Boulton Publishing Services Inc.
Designed by Falcom Design and Communications Inc.
Printed and Bound in Hong Kong by Book Art Inc.

Canadian Cataloguing in Publication Data

Ivy, Bill, 1953-
  Close to home : a Canadian country diary

ISBN 1-895246-11-3

1. Zoology - Canada - Pictorial works. 2. Natural
history - Canada - Pictorial works. 3. Canada -
Description and travel - 1981-   - Views.
I. Title.

QL219.I88 1990   779 '. 32 '0971   C90-094553-2

STEWART HOUSE
481 UNIVERSITY AVENUE
TORONTO, ONTARIO, M5G 2E9

INTRODUCTION

FOR ABOUT EIGHT MONTHS OF THE YEAR, I live by a small lake not far from Algonquin Park. Within easy reach of my home there are two major climatic zones, three types of forest, - the coniferous, the northern and the southern hardwoods, and the largest concentration of fresh water in the world. In addition, two important bird migration routes converge here, making it a paradise for birdwatchers.

Wherever I go I am always thinking of what I might find should I return later that day or that year. Properly reading nature's signs and learning to take a closer look are essentials to observation. Half-eaten leaves, footprints, well-worn paths, tufts of fur caught on a twig or tree-hole entrance, scats, and animal remains are all good clues as to what an area has to offer.

This book is the result of years spent observing and studying nature in the wild. Yet most of what I see is never captured on film. Often I put my camera down and simply watch. At other times the lighting is not right and I won't even attempt photography. Seeing a wild animal in its natural environment is always the great thrill. To capture it on film is simply a bonus.

Since seasons vary from year to year, the cycles of nature are not always predictable. However, I have found it is possible to forecast with a fair amount of accuracy what I can expect to see and when within a certain area. This book follows a typical year in my 'neck of the woods', so to speak. It would take volumes to include everything that I see and photograph in a year, so I included only a few select subjects that have become very familiar to me. While not everyone is fortunate enough to live in such a bountiful area as I do, there is an endless variety of flora and fauna almost anywhere. You need not travel far - your backyard, the city park or a country lane can offer just as many opportunities for discovery as far-off exotic lands.

For the past 15 years I have kept a nature diary in which I record each day's sightings. Although I do travel on occasion, my preferred method of nature study and photography is to work one area intensively rather than simply to visit a place for a week or so. The renowned naturalist Louis Agassiz once said, 'I spent the summer travelling, I got halfway across my backyard.' There is much more to be seen and discovered in one's own 'backyard' than there is time to see it. And there are many advantages I derive from staying 'close to home'. The animals around me often become familiar friends. I get to know the same pairs of nesting loons, geese and herons as well as successive generations of foxes, racoons, squirrels, and hares. Each year I visit favourite stands of orchids and other wildflowers. These personal 'gardens' require no tending and bring me much more pleasure than any city arboretum ever could.

While out in the field I am always on the lookout for new discoveries. Nature never stands still, so each month offers something new and exciting. By becoming familiar with the different environments around your own place you will become much more successful at locating specific species. A field of milkweed in July will almost certainly yield a few monarchs, just as a sphagnum bog in June is a good bet for orchids. Reading up on the subjects you are

SPRING BUDS

interested in will greatly increase your chances of finding them in the wild. For example there's no point looking for gentians in May or moose in an area overrun with deer. But a patch of jewel-weed that is immature in early summer may be an ideal spot to return to later on if you enjoy watching hummingbirds, as is an apple orchard in the autumn dusk if you wish to see deer or bears.

There are always new horizons awaiting us, regardless of our age or experience in the wilds. The more we learn the greater our appreciation and respect for the natural world becomes. Hopefully this book will serve to show that the wonders of nature, with its ever-changing seasons and landscapes, are available to everyone, and worthy of our protection.

BILL IVY

A P R I L

F OR THE MOST PART,

April lives up to its reputation as the rainy month.

But the showers do wonders for the grasses,

for the wildflowers and the shrubs. Signs of new

life are everywhere. Spring migrants arrive in earnest

and the battle over territorial boundaries begins.

Many birds are already on the nest. The woods

and fields are no longer silent but resound with the

sound of the birds. Lakes, rivers and ponds open up

and once again teem with life as both the reptiles and

amphibians begin their spring courtships.

CANADA GOOSE *Branta canadensis*

PRIL *11* On the morning this first picture was taken I woke to a fierce spring blizzard. I hadn't planned on going out with the camera, but I was worried about a pair of Canada geese who were nesting in a nearby marsh so I headed out. I knew the female was sitting on a full clutch of eggs because I had photographed her there the week before. Visibility was really poor, and when I first spotted the nest I thought it was abandoned. All I could see was a mound of snow, but once I got a little closer, sure enough, a head popped out. I quickly snapped a couple of shots and backed off. Keeping a close eye on

CANADA GOOSE *Branta canadensis*

me was the gander, swimming by himself in the nearby pond. The snow was still coming down heavily and it continued to bury the goose when I left for home.

All the same, three weeks later seven healthy goslings hatched and I was lucky enough to be there. When you are photographing goslings on the nest timing is very important. They stay at the nest for only one day and then they leave with their parents and never come back to the nest again. They do stay in the marsh - in a way the whole marsh is their home - and the mother shelters them at night beneath her body.

After wintering in the southern United States and Mexico mated pairs of Canada geese return to their favourite nesting grounds. The pair will usually remain together for life. This is one of the few species of birds in which the family unit remains together for almost a full year. Four to six eggs are incubated by the female alone, while the male stands guard close by. The goslings are able to feed themselves, swim and even dive very soon after birth. Their watchful parents never let them out of their sight. After two months the young geese will weigh about three kilos or seven pounds; that's 24 times their birthweight.

The porcupine, or 'quill pig' as it is also known (overleaf), can weigh up to 13 1/2 kilos or thirty pounds. It has poor eyesight and if you approach quietly you can

A P R I L 15

often get to within a few feet before being seen. This living pincushion is covered with more than 30,000 needle-sharp quills which can be lethal weapons. Each quill is actually a hardened hair with tiny barbs on its tip. The porcupine cannot in fact fire these sharp needles at its enemies, as is commonly believed, but as it thrashes its tail back and forth to defend itself, many quills do accidentally fly off and land on the ground. Once while I was positioning myself for a ground-level shot of one of these animals I knelt in some of its discarded quills. Considering how much that smarted I shudder to think how a mouthful of them must feel, not to mention how dangerous it is. Animals as large as a bear have actually been killed in this way since they were no longer able to eat. Once a porcupine quill gets in the skin it is very difficult to remove. The barbs swell when moist and the quill gradually works its way in further and further.

In the spring, the porcupine gives birth to a single cub or 'porcupette'. Luckily for the mother, it is born with soft, pliable quills which do not harden till after they dry. Considering the size of its parent, the porcupine is

Porcupine *Erethizon dorsatum*

huge, about 30 centimetres or one foot long and weighing about half a kilo or one pound or so. That's larger than a bear cub at birth! The young porcupine matures quickly and can climb a tree within a couple of days. Although it is nursed by its mother for up to two months, the porcupette begins eating plant material in as early as a fortnight. By the fall it will head out on its own.

Among the early spring flowers is the sharp-lobed hepatica, a member of the buttercup family. You have to look quite carefully to spot the young plant among the  dried leaves on the forest floor. Its flowers range in colour from a deep lavender to a pale pink or white, and as the plant matures they may stand up to 23 centimetres or nine inches off the ground. Oddly enough, new leaves do not appear until after the flowers have bloomed.

The name hepatica means 'pertaining to the liver' since its leaves supposedly resemble the shape of our liver. I hope my liver never looks like that! In days past a medicine for liver trouble was made from its leaves.

SHARP-LOBED HEPATICA   *Hepatica acutiloba*

BLANDING'S TURTLE *Emydoidea blandingi*

PRIL *19* I remember seeing a lot more Blanding's turtles when I was young than I do today. In fact as a child I kept one for a pet for a while before returning it to the wild. Unfortunately this gentle-natured turtle is now considered an endangered species. It is found mainly in southern Ontario. The bright yellow throat makes it easy to identify. The helmet-shaped shell is about 20 centimetres or eight inches long, and hinged on the bottom. It is known as the 'semi-box turtle' because it cannot close up as tightly inside its shell as a box turtle, but still it is well protected should it find itself in trouble. When disturbed it hisses quite loudly.

The Blanding's turtle is mainly aquatic but may venture on land searching for insects or snails. It is very shy, and at the first sign of danger will dive underwater. This hardy turtle is very tolerant of the cold. I've even seen it swimming in a pond that was partially covered with ice.

PRIL *21* By the time the pussywillows bloom the male goldfinches are well on their way to wearing once again their beautiful lemon-yellow coats. The dull olive-yellow winter plumage will be completely replaced by the end of the month and usually well before. The cheery canary-like song of the goldfinch is perfectly suited to the few sunny days of April that I long for each year.

Aмerican Goldfinch *Spinis tristis*

The goldfinch (previous page) or 'wild canary' as it is often called, is a seed eater, though berries and insects do round out its diet. It travels in little groups across the countryside, and is easily recognised by its undulating flight. It is not a large bird, averaging only about 10 to 12 centimetres or four or five inches in length. I once discovered one of these lightweight finches caught in a burr. Unable to free itself it had died. Some have even been known to be trapped in spiders' webs. But that is a note I should not even sound at this joyous time of year. April for birds, animals and flowers is the month of new beginnings. Life starts afresh. April is a month of rebirth.

 **PRIL 29** Up until I found this young woodcock the only view I ever got of this species was the tail end as it exploded into the air, usually a mere few feet away from me. Few birds are as difficult to find in the field as this one. I once stalked a woodcock that I watched land in the woods and was very pleased that I was able to capture this master of camouflage on film, until I developed my film and discovered I had only a perfect picture of a rock.

 **A**MERICAN WOODCOCK *Philohela minor*

The woodcock or 'timberdoodle' is a strange bird indeed. Its eyes are so far back on its head that it can see a full 360 degrees, actually seeing better behind itself than in front. This enables it to be always on the lookout as it probes the earth with its long bill searching for earthworms. Not only does the woodcock use its bill to sense the movement of worms under the soil, but it can also grasp them by lifting the end portion of its upper mandible while keeping the rest shut tight. Usually its own weight in earthworms is eaten each day.

Often there is still snow on the ground when the woodcock arrives in the north. An average of four young are born each spring.

Some years I see very few tiger swallowtails, yet in other years they seem to be everywhere. These large butter- flies often feed together in groups, and are regular

A P R I L 30

visitors to both wild and garden flowers. They spend the winter hibernating as chrysalids, and often emerge by early April. There is regularly more than one brood a year.

Almost as interesting to me as the adult butterfly is its caterpillar. About five centimetres or two inches long, it has a pair of large orange and

Tiger swallowtail *Pterourus glaucus*

black false eyespots that seem to stare right back at you. Perhaps by looking a lot like a small green snake, it makes its enemies hesitant to attack. But should that not work the larva resorts to chemical warfare, giving off a strong odour from special horned-shaped scent glands behind its head. This has been described by some as a musky scent but to me it smells sickeningly sweet.

TIGER SWALLOWTAIL *Larva*

MAY

MAY IS SPRING'S BUSIEST MONTH

The spring migration is all but over and nesting is in

full swing. The trees are in full leaf, wildflowers

carpet the woods and butterflies and moths

are on the wing. The air is filled with sweet smells.

The last frost of the season gives way to mild,

sunnier weather. But May also brings the

pesky blackfly, bane of the north.

LARGE-FLOWERED TRILLIUM *Trillium grandiflorum*

May is the month of trilliums. Shady or moist woods are the best place to find these attractive flowers. Their name comes from the Latin 'tri', meaning three. Everything about these plants occurs in threes, sepals, petals, and a three-part pistal.

The first trillium to bloom and the largest is the large-flowered variety, (*trillium grandiflorum*) Ontario's floral emblem. The plant grows up to half a metre tall or about 18 inches and its flower may measure 10 centimetres or about four inches across. Deer browse on its buds and the Indians chewed its rootstalks as a cure for snakebite and other ailments. Once picked it may not bloom again for another seven or eight years. The large-flowered

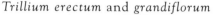
Trillium erectum and *grandiflorum*

Trillium grandiflorum

Trillium erectum

trillium is often subject to infection by organisms which can cause a green stripe down the centre of each petal.

Smaller than the large-flowered species is the liver-red purple trillium (*trillium erectum*). This foul-smelling flower grows on a short stalk, and attracts small flies that act as pollinators. Because it blooms when the robins have returned it is known as the 'wake-robin'.

My favourite variety is the painted trillium (*trillium undulatum*) which blooms a bit later than the others. It has wavey-edged petals and a beautiful crimson-red centre. When young its leaves have a bronze tint to them. The painted trillium is not only to be found in the woods, but may be found growing in bogs as well.

Trillium undulatum

Woodchuck or Groundhog *Marmota monax*

M A Y 1

Finding this young groundhog was no accident. I had been coming to the den every day, hoping to be there when the young first ventured out. That is the best time to photograph them because they don't seem to have any fear and are very curious. This little chap was the first to appear. He was so tame I didn't even need to set up a blind. I was obviously the first creature other than his own family that he had ever seen and he didn't quite know what to make of me. He was only one of four youngsters taking turns peeking out at the strange big animal - me - lying face down in front of their den. It wasn't until their mother found out what they were up to that the photo-session ended. I waited close to two hours more but they never showed their faces again. Mom must have taught them their first lesson, never to play with strangers.

The largest member of the squirrel family, the woodchuck or groundhog spends the winter in deep hibernation. The summer and early fall are spent storing up fat for the long winter ahead. The family will often hibernate together and then split up the following year. During its long winter sleep the woodchuck's body becomes stiff and cold, its temperature drops to just above freezing, its heart slows from 100 to four beats a minute, and it only breathes once every six minutes. Despite the February 2 legend of 'Groundhog Day' it rarely emerges from its den before mid-March. Sometime in the early spring, two to five young are born. Naked and blind at birth, they are only ten centimetres or four inches long. However they grow quickly and are weaned when about six weeks old. Then they start venturing outside their den, and begin feeding on the grass and green plants close by. Woodchucks love the sun, and are often to be seen basking in its warm rays in front of their den. They are good climbers, and many times I have seen them up a tree nibbling on its leaves.

M A Y 8

By early May, male American toads (overleaf) have usually arrived at their breeding grounds and begin calling to attract females. Their loud trill is really quite musical and can last for up to 30 seconds. They sing by passing air over their vocal chords, the sound resonating in their balloon-like throat sac. To get this photo I slowly crawled into the water beside the toad and began what I thought were very bad toad-trill imitations. Usually a toad will not call if it knows that a human being is nearby, but to my surprise this obviously lovesick toad responded to me. I was pleased to get my picture, but happier still that no one was around to see me in a pond on my hands and knees, singing face to face with a toad. It is best for a naturalist to work alone.

AMERICAN TOAD *Bufo americanus*

After breeding in a pond or marsh, this prolific toad lays up to 8000 eggs in long strings of jelly attached to underwater plants. The jet-black tadpoles hatch within a fortnight and transform into tiny replicas of their parents in about two months. Contrary to popular belief, one cannot get warts from handling a toad. However, toads do have a gland behind each eye which does secrete a poison strong enough to sicken a predator.

The American toad eats an incredible number of insects. It has been estimated that under normal conditions a toad consumes as many as 10,000 insects in just twelve weeks. No wonder farmers welcome these natural pest-controllers into their gardens. Toads capture their prey with a quick flick of the tongue, much faster than the human eye.

EASTERN COTTONTAIL *Sylvilagus floridanus*

If you want to find a nest of young cottontails you practically have to stumble over them, it is so well camouflaged. The doe digs a shallow hole in the ground and lines it with grass and some of her own fur. Into this soft cradle an average of four young are born. If, as is often the case, they are born somewhere else, the litter will be carried back to the nest one by one.

M AY 10

The mother then covers them with a warm blanket of more grass and fur and stands watch close by. At night she returns to nurse her babies, but never hovers over them just to keep them warm. From dusk to dawn they are left alone. The blind and naked youngsters grow very quickly. In one week they are covered in fur and before the end of a fortnight venture out of the nest. For the next few days they stay close to home, each little rabbit having its own special place under a bush or a plant, or in the grass. For a short while they all return to sleep together in the nest, but once things get too crowded they move out for good.

In a short ten weeks the cottontails reach adult size, and they will start raising families of their own after six months. In the meantime their mothers will have already had at least two more litters, which is no wonder, since a doe may mate again before her young are even one day old.

MAY 28

There is a heronry about six kilometres or three and a half miles from my place and I visit it every year. It's not easy to get to though, there's no path in and the woods are thick and tangled, but once you get there it's certainly worth the effort. But at this time of year the place is really buzzing and not just with herons! The mosquitoes and blackflies are almost unbearable. I try to protect myself by wearing musk-oil, a bug jacket, head net, hip-waders and even gloves, and yet I always come home with about 40 blackfly bites alone, never mind all the rest. Some 60 herons nest here. The sky above is like an airport, with birds constantly landing and taking off. The adults and young always seem to be squawking at each other and it's so noisy you can hardly hear yourself scratch. At this age the young are rarely left alone and both parents take turns bringing food to the nest. I snapped this picture seconds before dinner arrived. Then the fight began as to who got fed first.

In early spring the great blue herons return to their breeding grounds from the south. The nest is a bulky platform of sticks and is usually built in a dead tree, sometimes as high as 40 metres or 130 feet off the ground. They are communal nesters, with as many as a hundred or more pairs sharing the same heronry. Dozens of nests may be built in the same tree, each one containing an average of four eggs. The parents take turns feeding regurgitated food to the nestlings for the next two months or so. Should one of the youngsters fall out of the nest it may not survive since the adults will ignore its cries for food. Once their young have left the heronry, the parents go their separate ways.

Great Blue Heron *Ardea herodias*

The great blue heron is the best known and most widely distributed heron in North America. Formerly hunted for its attractive head-plumes, it is now a protected species.

Silk Moths Family *Saturniidae*

Late May is the time when appear our grandest insects, the silk or emperor moths. These incredibly beautiful creatures are truly works of art. Their size is impressive - some have a wingspan of over 15 centimetres or six inches and in flight they are often mistaken for bats. Their bodies are quite stout and are covered with thick fur.

If you have never seen a silk moth before, there is good reason. Not only are most species active only at night, but the adult insect lives for only a week or two. As adults none of them have any mouth-parts for feeding. They die of starvation shortly after mating and laying their eggs. Most spend the winter as chrysalids either in silken cocoons or underground.

Also known as the robin moth, the cecropia (*Hyalophora cecropia* overleaf) is the largest member of its family. The male is easy to identify by his long, plume-like antennae, which are sensitive enough to pick up the perfume or pheromone of the female for a radius of up to five kilometres or three miles. Should you happen to find a female, try putting her in a screened cage outdoors for an evening and if there are any males around they will surely find their way to her. The female cecropia lays between 200-300 eggs on a variety of leaves.

CECROPIA *Hyalophora cecropia*

The cecropia caterpillar, which is covered with many colourful tubercles, spins a large cocoon attached to a twig sometime in August. The adult moth usually emerges the following spring but sometimes holds out for an extra year. Once the leaves are off the tree these cocoons are easy to spot. I usually have no trouble finding a half-a-dozen or so each year.

The polyphemus (*Antherea polyphemus* opposite) is named after the one-eyed cyclops in Homer's *Odyssey* for an obvious reason, the large eyespots on its hind wings. The polyphemus is the most common of all our silk moths, and is on the wing from early June into July. Its accordian-shaped caterpillar has the distinction of being listed in the *Guiness Book of World Records* as being the most prodigious eating-machine in the world. In the first 48 hours of its life it eats an amazing 86,000 times its own birthweight. That's like a three kilo or seven pound baby taking in 269 tons of pablum. When full-grown and ready to pupate, the larva spins a tough, leaf-wrapped cocoon, which usually falls to the ground in the fall. There were once plans to use its silk commercially but it proved to be not a continuous thread and therefore of no use.

The magnificent luna moth (*Actias luna* overleaf) proves that the tropics do not surpass our own continent when it comes to insect beauty. It is a masterpiece of symmetry and grace. Only found in North America, it prefers thickly wooded areas. When exposed to sunshine, even for a short while, its colour quickly fades to a yellowish-grey. While here in the north

MALE CECROPIA *Hyalophora cecropia*

POLYPHEMUS *Antherea polyphemus*

Polyphemus *larva*

the outer margins of its wings are always yellow, southern species are rimmed with pink or red in the spring. The luna's jade-coloured larva spins a thin cocoon, often with a leaf attached to it. Females will mate, lay eggs and die,while never having gone far from the empty cocoon. Because its numbers have been so depleted by pesticides and pollutants, the luna moth is now considered an endangered species.

Luna *Actias luna*

J UNE

J UNE BRINGS IN THE SUMMER,
and with it the summer solstice, the longest day
and the shortest night. In meadows and fields
wildflowers abound, while in the shady woods they
gradually thin out. Bogs and marshes are in
full bloom. Young animals venture out of their
dens for the first time, and the birds are busy raising
their young. Butterflies and moths begin laying
their eggs and reptiles bask in the sun.

SHOWY LADY'S-SLIPPER *Cypripedium reginae*

ORCHIDS

June is the month for orchid lovers, and who isn't one? There is a mystique about these plants which captivates the imagination. The Great Lakes region of Ontario has been blessed with many of the most showy specimens in all of North America and without a doubt I have expended more time and energy searching for orchids than for anything else in the natural world.

To me the queen of all our native orchids is the showy lady's-slipper (*Cypripedium reginae*). Growing to a metre or 36 inches high, it is found in open areas around the margins of bogs, swamps and moist woods. Each plant produces up to four generous pink and white 'slippers'. Its leaves and stems are covered with coarse hairs that give some people a rash similar to poison ivy. Unfortunately this has not prevented overpicking which, along with the widespread destruction of wetlands, has contributed to its decline in many areas.

ARETHUSA *Arethusa bulbosa*

The smaller but no less impressive arethusa (*Arethusa bulbosa*) grows to a height of 25 centimetres or 10 inches. This bizarre-looking plant is also known as 'the dragon's mouth' for obvious reasons. Its colourful crested lip acts as a landing runway for bees and other insects that this plant relies upon for pollination. The arethusa blooms in swampy margins of my lake. An especially nice grouping was flattened one year by a pair of nesting loons.

SMALL YELLOW LADY'S-SLIPPER *Cypripedium pariflorum*

The small yellow lady's-slipper (*Cypripedium pariflorum*) blooms in bogs, moist woods and swamps. One of several varieties of yellow lady's-slipper, this particular one is distinguished by its smaller size and long, purplish-brown spirally-twisted side petals. Its dainty pouch has a very fragrant aroma. It bears from three to five leaves with very pronounced parallel veins.

You can find the pink lady's-slipper (*Cypripedium acaule*) in a wide variety of habitats, including both hardwood and conifer woodlands, bogs, and swamps. I once found a few of them growing in a graveyard. If you are fortunate you may find several hundred of these orchids in a small, select area. It takes up to 15 years for the pink lady's-slipper or moccasin flower to grow from a seed to a flowering plant. Insects, like the bumblebee, are drawn to its colourful pouch but once inside find no nectar and leave unrewarded. However, enough of them visit to ensure pollination.

Pink Lady's-Slipper   *Cypripedium acaule*

COMMON LOON *Gavia immer*

JUNE 4 Some pictures you really work for, others are a gift and this was one of them. I discovered this nest while I was out walking along the side of a nearby lake. It was only about 10 metres or 30 feet from the shore and in full sunlight. After taking a few shots from dry land I slowly waded out with my camera and tripod into the water. It took about 20 minutes to work my way in to chest level. The water was rather chilly since I wasn't wearing waders but my main concern was that I did not swamp my camera, it being a very windy day. The picture was taken with the camera no more than a few centimetres above the water level. I waited a long time to get that highlight in the eye.

A week or so later a pair of chicks were hatched. If only all loon nestings were as successful. The year before I had been working a nest in a rather remote area. As I approached by canoe to photograph hatchday I was shocked to find the decapitated body of the loon beside its eggs. I later learnt this was the work of a great horned owl, probably the same one I heard calling the night before. Supposedly this is a nasty habit some of them have, taking the heads off nesting ducks.

Few sounds in nature stir the emotions like the haunting call of the loon. The American Indians believed its wail meant that rain was on the way. Although it can hardly walk on land without falling on its face, the loon is perfectly suited for life in the water. Its feet are set well back on its body, which is a great advantage when diving. Unlike those of most water birds, the bones are filled with solid marrow, of a density that enables the loon to sink quickly underwater and it can store enough oxygen in its body to remain underwater for up to five minutes at a time.

The loon builds its nest at the water's edge, usually on an island. As a rule two eggs are laid and incubation is shared by both sexes. Soon after the chicks hatch the nest is abandoned. To help keep their downy feathers from becoming waterlogged, young loons often hitch rides on their parents' backs, but by the time they are two weeks old they are already skilled swimmers and divers. Come the fall, the family migrates south together.

JUNE 5

A member of the buttercup family, the wild columbine (overleaf) grows up to one metre or three feet tall. It is a favourite of hummingbirds, whose long beaks enable them to feed on the nectar deep within the tubes. Other insects drill holes directly into these spires to get at the sweet liquid.

Wild columbine grows in woodlands and shady rocky areas. For this reason the scarlet flowers are nicknamed 'rock bells'. However to me they will always be the 'honeymoon wreckers'. While photographing these blossoms I became so absorbed in what I was doing that I was oblivious to the many plants rubbing against me. It was an exceptionally hot day, so I wasn't wearing a shirt, a big mistake when you are working in a poison ivy patch. The next day I was covered in rashes, and spent the rest of my honeymoon scratching.

JUNE 7

There is nothing I enjoy more than sitting in a field of wildflowers and watching the ruby-throats darting from blossom to blossom (page 31). If you sit perfectly still they rarely notice you at all. Masters of flight, when hovering they beat their wings 55 times a second, and as many as 75 times a second when flying straight ahead. Because of their high metabolism they must feed every 10 or 15 minutes, all day long. At night they go into a stupor. They could starve to death overnight if they didn't. The sexes are easy to tell apart because

WILD COLUMBINE *Aquilegia canadensis*

RUBY-THROATED HUMMINGBIRD *Archilochus colubris*

only the males have the iridescent throat-patch which actually looks black until the light illuminates it.

Despite its small size (about seven and a half centimetres or three inches) the ruby-throat bravely defends its territory and will even divebomb an eagle that dares to trespass. Occasionally you see one battling with a bumblebee over a choice flower. Life can be dangerous for these tiny birds. They must avoid spider webs and burrs, and a few unfortunate ones have been caught by the praying mantis. There are even reports of frogs snatching them out of the air. Of all the hummingbirds the ruby-throat makes the longest migration, an amazing 3200 kilometre or 2000 mile flight to the southern United States and Mexico.

Racoon Family *Procyon lotor*

J U N E **10**

Finding wild animals is one thing, capturing them on film is another, especially if they are six metres or 20 feet above the ground. After discovering this family of racoons in a tree hole I had to work out a way to get up to their level without disturbing them. Once they climbed up inside the tree to sleep I got to work. After strapping two extension ladders together and securing them with guide ropes, I tied my tripod and camera to the top and waited for the racoons to reappear. I was about five metres or 16 feet away from the den and waited a long two hours or so before the racoons finally showed their faces. At first they were wary of this strange figure hiding behind the camera, but in time they ignored me and went about their business so long as I didn't move. I was fortunate enough to photograph the kits nursing, a sight seldom seen. Needless to say by the end of a day stuck on those ladders I was so stiff I could hardly move.

The racoon is probably the most intelligent animal in North America. After raising two orphan racoons as a child I know first-hand what they are capable of - opening jars, turning on water taps for a drink, and pulling the plug out of the wallsocket while I was listening to music were common occurrences. I even watched one fellow turn on a fan during a hot spell and lie stretched out on his back in front of it to cool off.

Racoons mate in the winter and by April or May an average of four kits are born, usually in a hollow tree or log. However I have seen a family emerge from an abandoned groundhog hole. The kits are born blind but furred. Their eyes open in about three weeks. By the end of two months they venture out with their mother searching for food. They will spend the winter with her before going off on their own in the spring.

RACOON KIT

R ED FOX *Vulpes vulpes*

J UNE *12*

This was a day that I'll never forget. I was busy photographing a muskrat in the morning when I heard a loud shrill whistle. I knew it was a groundhog in some sort of trouble so I went to see what the fuss was about. By the time I got there it was too late for him, poor fellow, he was lying spread-eagled on the ground. Whatever had killed him had left but I knew it would be back sooner or later, so I decided to wait. It didn't take long. I heard a rustle in the bushes behind me and when I turned around there was a fox only a few paces away, staring right at me. I

took a couple of quick camera shots thinking that would scare it off. Instead it came up and sat right beside me. As usual I had run out of film. Rummaging through my pockets for more I took out my bible (I never leave home without it) and put it down on the grass. I couldn't believe it, that crazy fox just picked up the bible in its mouth, carried it away, dropped it, turned, and looked back at me again. The teeth marks are right there to this day bitten into the binding. When I threw down my empty film container in front of the fox, it did the same thing again, picked up the container, stalked off, dropped it, turned, stared and came back to me. Not until I stood up to go myself did the fox leave my side.

Later in the day I went back to the meadow to check on the groundhog. There was that same fox sitting over it. This time it was none too pleased to see me and for good reason. In the distance I could hear the whimpering cry of the hungry kits.

I realized that the business with the bible and the film container had all been a way of distracting me from the den. So I stayed well back but kept on shooting as the fox sectioned up the kill. When it trotted off with the meat it left in completely the opposite direction from the den, hoping again to divert me. Not wanting to bother it anymore I simply headed home myself.

Usually shy and nervous, the red fox is seldom seen. Yet it is the most widely distributed carnivore in the world and lives in a variety of habitats. Thought to be quite intelligent, it has a well-earned reputation for cunning.

RED FOX *Vulpes vulpes*

It will eat almost anything, and devours more mice than any other creature on earth.

Red foxes mate in the winter, and by March or April the vixen gives birth to an average of four or five cubs in a grass-and-leaf-lined den. The male may or may not assist with the raising of the young. By the time they are two months old the kits are weaned and learning how to fend for themselves, and by the end of the summer the family members go their separate ways.

COW MOOSE AND TWINS *Alces alces*

JUNE 24

A good photograph usually requires a great deal of concentration. Some days I get so involved in my work that I take chances I would not ordinarily take. This morning was one of them. I discovered a cow moose and her twins (previous page) feeding by a lake in Algonquin Park, one of the best places in the world to see moose in the wild.

After taking a few boring pictures of this family from a hill, I decided the only way to get worthwhile shots was to take them from waterlevel. I slowly worked my way down to the edge of the pond and hid behind some shrubs. I set up my tripod and started taking pictures, edging closer and closer to my subjects every few minutes. After 20 minutes or so I was right at the water's edge, still partly hidden but no more than 12 metres or 40 feet away. I was sure they did not know I was there but immediately after I took this photo all eyes turned on me. The next thing I saw through the lens was the cow moose charging. I grabbed my camera and tripod and stumbled through the bushes. I never looked back until I reached the top of the hill. Looking down I saw her standing by the edge of the water. Her charge was probably a bluff but I was not about to return and find out.

The moose is our largest deer. A large male can stand over two metres or six feet tall at the shoulder and weigh up to 650 kilos or 1400 pounds. His rack can measure nearly two metres across. Females are much smaller and do not grow antlers. Despite its size, a moose can move as quietly as a cat through the woods.

By the end of May or early June, a single calf is born. However an older cow may give birth to twins or more rarely triplets. Helpless at birth, a calf can swim and outrun a human being within a few days. Young moose grow quickly, gaining up to a kilo or about two pounds a day for the first month of life, and up to two and a quarter kilos or five pounds a day after that right until the fall. They will stay with their mother for a year or more. Once the cow is ready for her next calf they are driven away to fend for themselves.

J U L Y

J ULY IS THE HOTTEST MONTH
of the year. It produces dramatic thunderstorms,
and warm, muggy nights alive with insects.
The days are long and sunny. Wild berries begin
to fruit on vines, trees and shrubs.
Thick vegetation and decreased activity make the
sighting of wildlife more of a challenge.

CAPE HARE *Lepus europaeus*

The original 'Easter Bunny', the Cape hare was introduced to New York state from Germany in 1893, and is now established in the Great Lakes region. Also known as the European hare, it prefers open areas, and is the largest hare within its range. During the mating season the males and females put on quite a show fighting amongst themselves. Sometimes they even stand on their hind legs and box it out. This is where the phrase 'as mad as a March hare' comes from.

JULY 1

The Cape hare's young, or leverets, are born in an uncovered nest, fully furred and with their eyes open. They do not all remain in the same nest, but rather are scattered into separate forms or individual nests. At night the mother makes her rounds, feeding each one in turn. Within a few days the leverets are almost able to look after themselves. Should their mother want to rally them together, all she has to do is call and they come running. Often several broods are raised a year.

CAPE HARE *Lepus europaeus*

WHITE ADMIRAL *Basilarchia arthemis*

JULY 7

Also known as the banded purple, this sun-loving butterfly is often to be seen sitting on a favourite perch, wings open to the warm summer rays. Without question one of our most beautiful butterflies, it is primarily found in open wood and forest edges. Should another butterfly or insect pass by it will often dart out at the trespasser. In addition to flower nectar, the white admiral also feeds on aphid honeydew, and frequently on carrion. Its caterpillar hibernates for the winter when partially grown, in a rolled-up leaf referred to as a 'hibernaculum'. The population of this species varies from year to year , and occasionally large numbers of these butterflies can be found in very small areas. One sight I'll never forget was a tree I found laden with more white admirals than I had ever otherwise seen in a single season.

J U L Y 15

I really enjoy a good thunderstorm, the more violent the better. This one was the best I've ever seen. It was 4:30 in the afternoon when the rumbling started. I was in the Georgian Bay islands, at one of my favourite spots. I headed for the beach and set up my camera and tripod. I could see the thunderheads forming out over the bay but it was fully dusk before the storm actually reached me. It was pouring and of course I wasn't wearing a raincoat, but I did cover my camera with a plastic bag and for the next few hours I stood in the rain trying to get as many lightning bolts on film as possible. It was nearly midnight when I finished the roll. By then the storm was directly overhead, one of those moments you never forget. There I was, actually standing at the water's edge of all places, with forks of lightning forming a purple dome all around me. Very dangerous - yet what a crowning glory. But the film was finished and I knew that I should get out while I could.

It is awesome to think that this was only one of some 1,800 storms of its kind that are going on somewhere or other around the world at any given moment. Lightning flashes strike the earth about 100 times a second as a result. Thunderstorms are a very important source of food for plants. The intense heat of the lightning fuses nitrogen from the atmosphere into nitrogen-oxide that is soluble in water. The rain then washes this into the soil, so providing nourishment for the plants.

LIGHTNING OVER GEORGIAN BAY

BLUE JAY *Cyanocitta cristata*

JULY 19

A member of the crow family, the blue jay is one of our most intelligent birds. It can skilfully mimic the call of many other species, and has been known to imitate the screech of a red-tailed hawk around other birds, sending them into a panic. On many occasions I have heard it echo the sound of my own squeaky clothesline. Like crows, blue jays seem to enjoy harassing roosting owls. However they themselves are often chased by smaller birds, and for good reason because they will not hesitate to rob a nest of eggs or young.

During the nesting season these usually noisy birds become very quiet. For some reason they often build a false nest of twigs before their actual nest is built. The nest is a bulky structure of twigs, moss and grass. Each stick used in the construction is tested before being added and weak ones are tossed aside. Four to six eggs are laid, and are usually incubated by the female alone. Blue jays are very protective of the nest and will not hesitate to divebomb any intruder, even on occasion a too-curious birdwatcher. The young are fed by both parents till they mature, at which time they will leave the nest to band together with other families.

It's safe to say the red squirrel doesn't like visitors. The minute you enter its territory the scolding begins. Chattering, barking and squealing from the safety of an overhead branch, the unhappy squirrel stamps its feet and jerks its tail in defiance. Even after you leave it still goes on grumbling to itself. American folklore says that it will chase and castrate any male gray squirrel that gets too close, but fortunately for the gray cousin only the first part of this belief is true.

J U L Y 23

The red squirrel inhabits a home-range of about a hectare, or two or three acres. Its young are born blind and helpless, in a tree cavity or leaf nest. They are weaned by the eighth week of life, at which time they venture outside the den for the first time. The few times I have been fortunate enough to observe their 'coming out' so to speak I have found them more curious of me than frightened, if only for a day or so. They are so frisky and playful at this stage that they are a joy to watch. Broods which are born in the spring often break up by early fall. If there is a second brood in late summer, that family will stay together over the winter.

RED SQUIRREL *Tamiascurus hudsonicus*

YOUNG GREAT BLUE HERON *Ardea herodias*

JULY 29 They don't call the great blue heron ' big cranky' for nothing. When I discovered this youngster it had just recently left the heronry and was surprisingly tame but very irritable.   I took these shots a mere arm's-length away. That was an exhilarating experience but rather dangerous, for a heron can strike a

pinewood oar with such force that its bill jabs right through and out the other side. Consider this my last wide-angle heron shot.

I spent the greater part of the afternoon watching this one hunt for frogs and minnows. Good fishing is obviously a learned skill, since the heron missed its strikes more often than not. However by late afternoon it had caught half a dozen frogs. That's a lot better than I did the day before at the same pond. I caught only one.

AUGUST

AUGUST IS UNPREDICTABLE.

*It can be hot, wet or dry. It is a month of
contrasts, when nature seems to be waiting for a
time of change. Early mornings are often
shrouded in mist but the crisp, clear nights are
ideal for star-gazing. The woods and fields can be
strangely quiet as the wildlife seems to have retreated.
Many birds are still moulting while others are
beginning to gather in flocks for their fall migrations.*

GREAT TIGER MOTH *Arctia caja americana*

Active only at night, the great tiger moth relies mainly on its senses of smell and hearing to find its way around. It has a very well-developed hearing

AUGUST 3

organ, or 'tympanum', on each side of its body, which can detect sounds far beyond the range of our ears. These include the high-frequency pulses of bats. The second the tiger moth realizes it has been detected by a bat's 'radar' it drops to the ground like a rock. The tiger moth has another defense against its enemies, a foul-smelling liquid which it emits when captured, a toxin that is usually enough to deter most predators. And again, the moth's bold markings act as a further reminder to stay away. Even to see one of these beautiful moths is a treat since it is quite rare in North America, yet where I live a few are drawn to my night-lights each year.

By the time most birds have finished nesting the cedar waxwing is just starting to build its nest. It seldom lays its eggs before late June or July.

AUGUST 9

There's a good reason for this. When the young hatch out the berry crop that feeds them is at its best. Waxwings love berries and sometime gorge themselves with so many that they can hardly fly. They also get drunk on occasion by eating over-ripe fruit. Hopefully they don't feed this food to their young too often. On average, four eggs are incubated by the female, who is fed on the nest by her mate. In just over two weeks the young will have left the nest.

CEDAR WAXWING *Bombycilla cedrorum*

Cedar waxwings mate for life, and when one partner dies the other may call in distress for as long as two days. Sometimes they have two broods a season, and will actually mate and build a new nest while they are still feeding their first family.

AUGUST *12*

Few people pass by the pitcher plant without taking a closer look. This bizarre carnivorous plant grows in bogs and spongy areas of coniferous forests. Its single yellow and dull-red flower dangles from the end of a long, stiff stem up to 60 centimetres or 24 inches tall. Insects attracted to its pitcher-shaped leaves crawl inside but have great difficulty escaping because of the numerous downward-pointing bristles holding them back. Eventually they drown in the liquid at the base of the pitcher. This mixture of rainwater and a sweet, sticky plant secretion digests the insect's body and provides the plant with much-needed nitrogen, so lacking in a bog environment.

Should you ever need a drink of fresh, uncontaminated water while out in the field keep the pitcher plant in mind. The water at the top of each 'vase' is said to be clear enough to drink, since the undigested hard parts of the insects settle at the bottom and can easily be avoided. This has earned the pitcher plant the nickname 'hunter's cups'. Thankfully, I have yet to be that desperate for a drink.

PITCHER PLANT *Sarracenia purpurea*

SOUTHERN FLYING SQUIRREL *Glaucomys volans*

UGUST *19* On moonlit summer nights I often sit out in the woods and watch the flying squirrels glide from tree to tree. These intriguing animals have a loose fold of skin joining their wrists and ankles which acts as a gliding wing and enables them to sail through the air for up to 45 metres or 150 feet. The higher the launch the further the glide. Their flattened tail serves as a rudder, allowing them to change direction in mid-flight. Graceful in the air, they are awkward and clumsy on the ground.

The southern flying squirrel's large bulging eyes are typical of many nocturnal species. During the day the squirrel sleeps in a tree cavity, usually an abandoned woodpecker hole or occasionally a leaf nest. Although they are rarely seen they are quite common. I have found that if you tap on enough hollow trees, eventually one of these squirrels will poke its head out to see what's going on.

UGUST *22* Just over five centimetres or two inches long, this attractive dragonfly is found near ponds and slow-moving rivers. Like other members of the skimmer family, its body is shorter than its wingspan. The four wings move independently of each other, enabling the dragonfly to move with mastery in any direction. They generate a lift of about seven times the insect's

Twelve-Spotted Skimmer *Libellulla pulchella*

bodyweight. That's almost five times as much as an aeroplane can command at best. Like all other dragonflies, this species cannot fold its wings against its body, and when at rest it keeps them out to the side. Each of its large eyes is a composite of nearly 20,000 units, which together give it close to 360-degree vision. Few insects can escape this skilful hunter, not even mosquitoes.

The twelve-spotted dragonfly nymph lives underwater and feeds on insects and tadpoles. Once fully grown it leaves the water. After splitting the skin down the back the adult dragonfly emerges, leaving an empty shell behind.

The sweet perfume of this elegant lily is a favourite of mine. The large waxy blossom, which opens in the early morning and closes shortly after noon, usually lasts no more than three days. Anchored to the bottom of ponds, marshes and lakes, the rootstalks may be a couple of metres long. Frogs, birds and dragonflies often use its floating leaves as a resting place. These lilypads are two-toned, shiny green on the top and purple underneath. The fruit is eaten by fish and mammals, and the seeds can be popped like popcorn. The plant is also known as the pond lily.

AUGUST 26

FRAGANT WATER-LILY *Nymphaea odorata*

AUGUST 28

The gray treefrog is seldom seen, since it spends most of its life in a shrub or tree. However, almost every year in late summer a few of these amphibians gather near or on my back window to feast on the scores of insects attracted to the porch light.

After breeding and laying its eggs in a shallow pond or stream, the gray treefrog returns to its arboreal life. An excellent climber, it has large adhesive disks on its feet. These 'suction cups' enable it to scale almost any surface, including a pane of glass. While it is normally gray or green, this master of camouflage can vary its colour from hour to hour depending on the temperature, light or setting. If you hear a loud musical trill on a hot summer's night it is more than likely one of these little minstrels announcing its presence.

COMMON GRAY TREEFROG *Hyla versicolor*

SEPTEMBER

SEPTEMBER SPELLS THE END OF SUMMER

with the autumn equinox, when day and night are
once more balanced. The golden harvest moon gives
way to chilly nights and frosty mornings.
Many animals are busy gathering food for the long
winter ahead. The landscape is once more alive with
birds as they begin their fall migrations.
Mushrooms sprout up and the year's last flowers
make their appearance. Splashes of colour dot the
landscape as the leaves begin to turn colour.

CARDINAL FLOWER *Lobelia cardinalis*

SEPTEMBER 7

There is a river flowing out the back of my lake which by the first week of September is lined with scores of cardinal flowers. Their colour is so brilliant that the banks seem to glow scarlet red, particularly on overcast days. A member of the bluebell family, the cardinal flower usually grows to about one and a quarter metres or four feet tall, but back there some are nearly as tall as I am. Hummingbirds are its main pollinators, partly because its deep narrow tubes make it inaccessible to bees. Sadly its great beauty has led to overpicking but it is now a protected species. In fact the cardinal flower was one of the first wildflowers taken back to England for use in gardens back in the time of the first Queen Elizabeth. The Indians used this plant to make cough medicine and a love potion.

CARDINAL FLOWER *Lobelia cardinalis*

Evening Primrose *Oenothera biennis*

 SEPTEMBER 11 True to its name, the evening primrose opens at twilight and closes by noon the next day. Night-flying moths, its main pollinators, are attracted by its lovely lemon fragrance. It takes two years for this plant to reach maturity. In the first year only its leaves appear and not until the following summer will it flower. Quite common wherever there is dry soil, this beautiful biennial grows up to 150 centimetres or five feet tall. The root of the evening primrose is edible if picked during the first year before the plant blooms. Its seeds, which grow in pods, are a favourite food of many birds. Although they first appear as early as June, I often see these flowers throughout the month of September.

SEPTEMBER 12 A late bloomer, the fringed gentian can sometimes be found shooting up from under autumn's fallen leaves. These beautiful flowers only grow where the soil and moisture conditions are just right. Look for them in moist meadows and along seepage slopes. Gentians love the sunshine, and fold up when the sky darkens. Growing up to 60 centimetres or two feet tall, mature plants may have many branches and dozens of blossoms, and range in colour from a light lavender to a deep

FRINGED GENTIAN *Gentiana crinita*

purple. Their exquisite fringed petals are not just for show, but rather act as a deterrent to many insect pests. When these try to crawl inside the flower, its delicate fingers collapse, dumping the intruders on the ground.

I once caught three short-tailed shrews (overleaf) in a live trap I had set for mice. About two hours later I checked up on

SEPTEMBER 18

them, and even though I had left them a few earthworms to eat, there was only one well-fed animal left. Not a single bone remained of the other two, only scraps of fur. It's a good thing this shrew is not much larger than my middle finger - if it were the size of a fox the woods wouldn't be safe. No other animal is as fierce and voracious for its size.Because of its high metabolism the short-tailed shrew must eat two or three times its own weight in food each day or it will die. This bizarre animal has musk glands and a venom in its saliva similar to that of a cobra. The toxin causes paralysis or death to animals as large as a vole. Should a human be bitten it will be some time before he or she will forget it.

The shrew is a study in perpetual motion, and is active year round. Its every movement is short, jerky and abrupt. It's no surprise to me that these highly-strung creatures usually burn themselves out in less than a year.

SHORT-TAILED SHREW *Blarina brevicauda*

SEPTEMBER 20 In nature photography, or when simply observing wildlife for that matter, planning ahead can really pay off. After listening to the weather report the night before, I was up and out in the field well before sunrise, hoping to photograph the season's first heavy frost. I was not disappointed, everything around me was covered in a beautiful white hoarforst. I headed to an area where I had seen numerous damselflies the day before, curious to find out what had happened to them overnight. To my surprise many of them were still there, trapped inside sparkling coats of ice. I selected this bluet as my model, since it was the most colourful and accessible. I had to work fast, well aware that frost melts much too quickly once the sun rises. Incredibly my captive subject thawed out before my camera's eye and flew off into the morning light. I wonder if that layer of ice didn't actually save its life, by insulating it from further chilling, much as a cranberry farmer may spray his crop with water the night before a frost.

Common Bluet *Enallagma ebrium*

SPOTTED SALAMANDER *Ambystoma maculatum*

S E P T E M B E R *29* The beautiful spotted salamander is rarely seen since it spends most of its life under leaves on the forest floor, or in underground tunnels and burrows. It is a member of the mole salamander family, which is unique to North America. Its yellow and orange spots are meant to warn predators of the toxins in its smooth, shiny skin. Supposedly after sampling one of these plump creatures an animal will avoid them in the future, however this isn't always the case since racoons are known to eat them regardless. The spotted salamander can measure over 23 centimetres or nine inches long, and can live up to 20 years. Like all amphibians, it never stops growing, and if it lived long enough it would be a monster.

Before the ground freezes in the fall these salamanders bury themselves deep in the earth and hibernate until the following spring. After breeding and laying their eggs in a pond, they return to their secretive, sluggish life on land. Once the larvae mature they too leave the pond.

S EPTEMBER 30

Few if any butterflies are as well known as the monarch. This is not surprising because its travel and migration habits are exceptional and the life-cycle is itself a wonder of nature. After hatching far away in the south of this continent, millions of these hardy insects head north. Although none of the first generation butterflies may get as far as Canada, their offspring will do so. The monarch lays its eggs singly on the underside of any plant of the milkweed family. After two weeks of almost non-stop eating its larva is about five centimetres or 2 inches long and ready to pupate. Attaching its rear claspers to a small silk button woven on a twig or leaf, the caterpillar then swings free and hangs upside down in the shape of the letter 'J'. After resting for a while it arches its back, forcing the skin to split open. Once it sheds this old coat it resembles a large, green water droplet. In a very short time the outer layer hardens into an elegant emerald case, decorated with gold. Inside this chrysalis there is nothing but a green liquid, from which the adult butterfly will be formed. Usually in about two weeks the chrysalis shell becomes transparent, revealing the adult butterfly

MONARCH *Danaus plexippus*

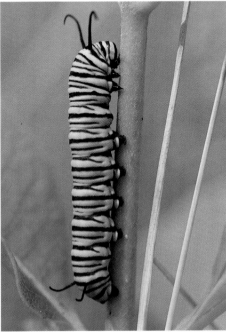

MONARCH *Danaus plexippus*

cramped inside. Next from within a tiny trapdoor is pushed open and a rumpled form tumbles out in a backward somersault. Clinging to its empty chrysalis, the newly-emerged insect begins pumping out as liquid from its swollen abdomen the stored wastes and unused substances of its former state. At the same time it begins to force body fluid into the wings along the channels that we call the 'veins'.

This expands the wings to their full size. They dry and harden in the open air and sun. We can better understand the veins if we think of them as flexible struts that support and manoeuvre the wing in flight. Circulation of fluid through these veins also helps to keep a stable body temperature.

In all it takes some 20 minutes before the perfect butterfly has finally reached its full size and beauty. I never tire of watching this miraculous transformation and each year, for my own delight, I raise a few monarchs from eggs found on the milkweed and release them back to the wild as soon as the adult insects emerge.

Monarchs may produce two or three broods a season. Come the fall they gather in large flocks and migrate south. The new generation of butterflies will follow the same route as did the previous year's migrants, resting at night on the same trees and heading always for the same destination. Many will have travelled over 3,000 kilometres or some 2,000 miles before reaching their wintering grounds on the southern coast of California or up in the Sierra Madre of central Mexico. There they will hang through the winter in clusters so dense and vast that they weigh down the trees and cover them like golden leaves.

A friend of mine tells me that back in about 1973 or 1974 he saw a migratory fly-past in Toronto of all places. One early autumn night he was sitting at dusk in his garden when suddenly the birds stopped singing and everything went still. Over the trees rose what looked at first like a small black cloud. It came on towards him, stretching out like a long flying carpet that revealed itself as it passed overhead to be a procession of hundreds of thousands of butterflies, all flying steadily southwest together, on and on for what seemed a long time. Then it was gone and the evening sky was empty once more. He moved away soon after and never saw it again. Anyway, urban sprawl and pollution would make such a sight unlikely in the city today.

Monarch *Danaus plexippus*

OCTOBER

OCTOBER IS A MONTH OF
breathtaking beauty. The trees are ablaze
with colour and their falling leaves decorate the
forest floor. But now the heavy frosts kill
off most of summer's insects as well as most of the
remaining wildflowers. Reptiles and amphibians
bury themselves in the mud and many animals are
busy topping up their caches and putting on weight
against the winter. The bird migration continues
and V's of honking geese still pass overhead.

BLACK BEAR *Ursus americanus*

There are a lot of black bears in the area where I live, and I go out looking for them at least two evenings a week. I discovered this one eating

OCTOBER 3

apples by the side of a road. It was late in the afternoon and by keeping myself between the low rays of the sun and my subject I was able to approach fairly close. Shortly after this picture was taken the bear headed back into the bush so I sat under a rock ledge and waited for its return. My wife, who was watching from afar with binoculars, started waving her hands and pointing at me. I assumed she was trying to tell me the bear had come back but still I saw nothing. It was not until I heard a rustling overhead that I stood up and startled the animal which took off at once. It had been peering down at me from a mere arm's length above.

The black bear is our most common, and is also our smallest, bear yet a large male can weigh up to 180 kilos or about 400 pounds. Females are much smaller, usually half the size of the male. Black bears have poor vision, but an acute sense of smell and hearing. In the fall they fatten up on fruits, berries, nuts and carrion in preparation for their long winter sleep. Contrary to popular belief they are not true hibernators, but rather enter a torpor, which is a state of lowered metabolism in which the temperature drops and the heartbeat slows, but to nothing like the same extent as hibernation.

COW MOOSE *Alces alces*

OCTOBER 6

The sun was just rising when I discovered this cow moose. She was busy browsing on a tree as I slowly approached her. As I got closer to her she timidly slipped behind a small shrub and peered around the leaves to get a closer look at me. It made me laugh to see such a large beast trying to hide behind such a small shrub. After we stared at each other for a while she let out a loud bellow that made me jump. My first thought was 'not a bad call' since I had been practising my own moose call all that week. She seemed very reluctant to leave, which surprised me until I heard another bellow from behind and realized that she had a visitor, a rather large male. Bull moose in the rutting season can be very dangerous and I was not too pleased to be caught between this amorous couple. Fortunately he was far enough away that I was able to get a few shots of him before I left. He was pawing the ground with his foot when I finally packed up my camera and dashed to the safety of my car.

I spent many nights watching this beaver go about his business. Almost every night for three weeks or so I would cross my lake by canoe and

OCTOBER 8

work my way through the woods to reach its lodge on the side of a riverbank. The beaver had dammed the river to form a surprisingly shallow pond to work in. I had heard that contrary to popular belief the beaver is not all that skilled a lumberjack. I can confirm that after watching this one fell a few trees. He obviously had no idea in which direction they would topple and more than one of them never even reached the ground. One particularly large poplar, with a diameter of at least half a metre, had him stumped, literally. Each time he tried to bring it down it would get caught in a nearby tree. Within a fortnight I counted at least two dozen pointed stumps at the base of this much shorter but still upright tree. Hoping to capture the action on film I built a natural blind within camera range. I returned that night and around two in the morning fell asleep while waiting for him to make an appearance. About two hours later I was awakened by the sound of chewing but it was so cold I could hardly move. The temperature had dropped close to freezing and my fingers were too numb to work the camera. By the time I warmed my hands my subject was gone. I never did get that shot but I was able to photograph this determined beaver eating leaves on a much more pleasant evening. By the way, that tree is still standing today.

BEAVER *Castor canadensis*

The beaver, our largest rodent, can reach lengths of up to one and a quarter metres or four feet and weigh as much as 27 kilos or 60 pounds. Still that's nothing compared to the giant beavers, two metres or six feet tall and 650 kilos or 800 pounds in weight, that once roamed this continent 10,000 years ago.

Well known for their dam-building skills, beavers also construct a network of canals for moving twigs and branches to their pond. In the fall they begin storing twigs underwater. Come winter this cache is retrieved from under the ice and taken into the lodge for food. Beavers are perfectly suited to their semi-aquatic life. Their coats are so waterproof that even after six minutes underwater their skin is still dry. Formerly hunted almost to extinction for their fur, these resilient animals are today more than holding their own.

OCTOBER *10*

The painted lady or cosmopolite is probably the most widespread butterfly in the world, and occurs in almost all environments, including alpine summits. It has a wingspan of about five centimetres or two inches and is a very strong flier. It is on the wing until the first hard frosts of autumn, and although it may migrate south for the winter, the parent butterfly does not make the return trip.

PAINTED LADY *Cynthia cardui*

SHAGGY MANE *Corprinus comatus*

The painted lady's spiny caterpillar is partial to thistle plants, which accounts for this species' other nickname, the 'thistle butterfly'. If there are any painted ladies in your area, it is likely you will find them at the nearest thistle patch laying eggs or feeding on the pink blossoms.

OCTOBER *14*

Every fall my wife picks a basketful of shaggy manes (previous page) and fries them for supper. She eats alone on those nights, and even though I realise they are a choice edible I have yet to try one. Maybe this year I shall. This distinctive mushroom is easily identified by its shape and shaggy cap, which has earned it the name 'lawyer's wig'. Despite its rather frail appearance, it can push up through asphalt. The shaggy mane grows in rows or clusters in grass or sandy soil. A member of the inky cap family, its gills auto-digest or deliquesce when mature, melting the cap into a black inky fluid.

OCTOBER *16*

I am very familiar with the deer mouse, a little creature with a long Latin name. We have shared the same residence for years now. Early in the fall they decide my place is more attractive than their own and try as I may I can't keep them out. I often live-trap them and move them to a new area, three or four kilometres away, since they have a strong homing instinct and can find their way back from any closer than that. Those few deer mice which do choose not to live inside with me begin storing tree-nuts and seeds in September for use in the winter. Like chipmunks they transport this food in their cheek pouches to a cache which may hold up to four and a half litres or a gallon of seeds. Occasionally cocoons, like those of the luna moth, are hidden away as well. Flowers, berries, insects and even the odd salamander or bird egg are also eaten when available.

Deer mice get their name from the colour of the coat, which often resembles that of a deer. They have a home range of about one and a quarter hectares or three acres and travel along well-beaten trails. When nesting they become very territorial, and will drive intruders away. Several broods are raised each year, which is a good thing since they are heavily preyed upon and rarely live longer than twelve months.

DEER MOUSE *Peromyscus maniculatus*

When I was finishing work on a previous book, my publisher said he needed an owl to round out the picture selection, and this was just two days

OCTOBER 23

before the book was due at the printer's. 'No problem,' I assured him as I left his office, not having the slightest idea where to find one that quickly, let alone get it on film. I decided to head out to the shore of Lake Ontario, hoping to find a late migrating saw-whet. I searched for hours and was about to quit for the day when I spotted a birdwatcher. Perhaps he had seen an owl or possibly he could direct me to a better spot? 'A month too late,' he regretted to inform me and chances were I wouldn't find one there anyway. After chatting for a while we said our goodbyes, when out of the corner of my eye I noticed what looked like a pair of yellow eyes staring at me. Sure enough, no more than a few steps away was this saw-whet owl (overleaf) who obviously overheard our whole conversation. I called to my fellow birdwatcher and pointed to the little bird perched in the cottonwoods. He nearly dropped his binoculars, we had a good laugh, and I got my picture. 'All in an afternoon's work,' I casually told my publisher when I left the picture on his desk the next day.

71

SAW-WHET OWL *Aegolius acadicus*

A mere 18 centimetres or seven inches tall, the saw-whet owl is North America's smallest owl. It gets its name from one of its unusual calls, which sounds like a saw being whetted or sharpened with a file. It roosts during the day in dense woodlands, but at dusk begins its hunt for insects, mice and birds.

This appealing little owl is often absurdly tame. Some have even allowed themselves to be caught by hand. Early in the autumn they begin their migration south, although many are permanent residents across the southern portion of Canada.

The smallest songbird in Canada, the golden-crowned kinglet (overleaf) is no more than 10 centimetres or four inches long. It nervously

OCTOBER 31

flicks its wings as it hops from perch to perch, searching for insects and their eggs. The patch on its head is orange with yellow borders in the male, and solid yellow in the female. This kinglet is also known as the 'goldcrest'. In the winter it commonly joins with flocks of chickadees and woodpeckers. I lured this bird into camera range by kissing the back of my hand and making a high, squeaky sound. Curiosity got the better of her and she immediately flew over to see who or what was calling. She showed very little fear of me, which is often the case with this species.

GOLDEN-CROWNED KINGLET *Regulus satrapa*

NOVEMBER

NOVEMBER LIES BETWEEN
autumn and winter. The trees are all but bare,
the leaves on the ground have lost their colour
and the landscape is a drab gray and brown.
The chilly, damp weather finally forces the
hibernators to retreat to their dens. The all-too-
fleeting days of Indian summer mark autumn's
last brave stand as the first snow flies. But the
bareness of the woods and meadows makes
this month one of the best for observing wildlife.

CLIMBING BITTERSWEET   *Celastrus scandens*

NOVEMBER 2

The attractive berries of the bittersweet are a favourite addition to dried-flower arrangements. Growing from a twining, woody vine, the small green flowers grow in terminal clusters about 10 centimetres or four inches long. They produce a yellow-orange fruit that ripens in the fall to a brilliant rosy-red. The berries are actually the plant's seeds. Although they are poisonous to many species, there are some such as rabbits, squirrels and songbirds that can eat them with no ill effects. Climbing bittersweet grows in woods, thickets and along riverbanks. If undisturbed its fruit remain throughout the winter.

NOVEMBER 12

No bird picks up my spirits like the chickadee, particularly when I'm out working in the middle of winter and a flock of them stops by looking for a handout. The woods wouldn't be the same without their cheery call. Permanent residents of southern Canada, they have an abundance of downy feathers, and are unperturbed by all but the coldest weather. In extreme temperatures they may sleep in tree holes rather than the usual thicket of coniferous trees. During this time of year chickadees must feed almost continuously, and will sometimes retrieve food collected months earlier and stored under loose bark. Winter flocks split up by the end of March.

BLACK-CAPPED CHICKADEE *Parus atricapillus*

EVENING GROSBEAK *Hesperiphona vespertina*

NOVEMBER *18*

There are few winter sights more impressive than a flock of these beautiful birds. The male at first glance looks a lot like an oversized goldfinch, except for the large or 'gross' beak which accounts for part of the name. Since they were once thought to come out of the woods to sing only after dusk, they were given their full name 'evening grosbeak'. We now know this is not the case but the name has stuck. Females are not as brightly coloured, but still are quite attractive.

Evening grosbeaks are relatively recent migrants from the west and were unknown in the east until about 1823. They are highly gregarious, even at nesting time. Mainly seed-eaters, they will battle it out among themselves for the best seeds at a feeding station when food is scarce in the winter.

GRAY WOLF *Canis lupus*

One of my earliest memories of the region is my calling to wolves in the early morning and having them answer. Twenty-five years

NOVEMBER 20

later I still hear them occasionally, and it is still thrilling. To me their haunting cries epitomize the wild. Wolves do not howl at the moon but rather at each other, sending information back and forth about their location, pack size, territorial boundaries, and intruders. Each wolf has its own unique voice when howling, much like we do when singing.

Seldom seen, the gray wolf is very shy, but is active all year round. It is mainly nocturnal and lives in well-organized packs that average between four to seven members. Led by a dominant male, the pack shares in the raising of the young and hunts as a unit. Moose and deer are their preferred diet in winter, but in other seasons they will often pursue easier game such as frogs, squirrels, rabbits and ground-nesting birds. They breed from February to March, and an average of five to seven young are born in an underground den about two months later.

DECEMBER

DECEMBER BRINGS THE WINTER SOLSTICE,
*the shortest day of the year. Many animals have now
changed into their white winter coats. The lakes and
ponds are frozen over and the odd snowstorm may
occur. The most obvious signs of animal life are the
many tracks through the snow. The annual migration
of birds has ended but the year-round residents are
still very much in evidence. This month is an ideal
time for searching out overwintering cocoons before
they are eaten by hungry animals.*

MOURNING DOVE *Zenaidura macroura*

DECEMBER 3

Named for its cry, the mourning dove (previous page) usually flies south for the winter. However some hardy birds choose to winter in southern Canada. During this harsh season they live in small flocks where seeds and tree cover are available, and sometimes roost on the ground. The flow of blood to their feet is sluggish in the cold weather and they have been known to lose several of their toes from freezing. Those doves that have migrated arrive back in the north sometime in March or April. The mourning dove mates for life.

DECEMBER 8

Also known as the wood mouse, this wide-eyed rodent is active all winter long. At this time of the year it may pair up with others of its kind although it usually does live alone. You sometimes see its tiny footprints on top of the snow, but most of the time it tunnels its way below the surface. Beneath this white, protective blanket the temperature usually remains above freezing. However mice are not always safe even under there because the fox is a master at sniffing and digging them out. During the winter the mouse relies heavily on its food cache from the previous autumn. If the weather becomes too extreme it may remain in its nest till things warm up.

WHITE-FOOTED MOUSE *Peromyscus leucopus*

WHITE-FOOTED MOUSE *Peromyscus leucopus*

The white-footed mouse is very difficult to distinguish from its relative the deer mouse, yet there are slight differences. As a rule it is not as large and spends much more time in trees. Its tail is usually shorter than its head and body and unlike that of the deer mouse the tail of the white-footed mouse is not always sharply bicoloured with a dark top and white bottom.

DECEMBER *17*

Almost every time I have seen a great horned owl I was alerted to its presence by the loud calls of its main antagonists, a flock of crows who just can't resist pestering any owl unfortunate enough to have its daytime roost discovered. Our largest tufted owl, this is a year-round resident of forests, swamps and open country. It is a fierce predator, rightfully earning itself the nickname 'tiger of the air'. It feeds on a wide variety of mammals, from those as small as a shrew to those as large and challenging as a porcupine. Geese, swans, ducks, hawks and other owls are just a few of the bird species it also preys on. Like others of its kind, the great horned owl flies almost silently thanks to special feathers which have soft, downy edges. With no whirring noise from its wings to interfere with its sensitive hearing, it can zero in on its prey and strike in almost total darkness.

The great horned owl hoots regularly during its winter courtship and is among the earliest birds to nest each year. By late February many are already on the nest in southern Canada. Usually an abandoned hawk, eagle, crow or squirrel nest is used. The heronry close to my place had a great horned owl occupy one of its nests for a couple of years at least.

GREAT HORNED OWL *Bufo virginianus*

DECEMBER *17*

A lot of people assume that the eastern gray squirrel hibernates during the winter, but that is not so. On particularly cold or stormy days it will remain in its nest, often with others of its own kind, otherwise it is active all season long. However, this can be a very difficult time of year for the gray squirrel, and it may even starve to death if the previous autumn's bounty of food proves to be insufficient. It digs down into the snow, looking for nuts stashed away weeks earlier, relying on its sense of smell to locate these valuable caches. Many are never found and therefore these animals contribute significantly to reforestation, because nuts otherwise left exposed on the forest floor could well end up being eaten by other animals rather than germinating.

Groups of squirrels formed over the winter usually break up in the spring. Unlike many squirrels, the gray is not overly protective of its own territory. The eastern gray squirrel raises two broods each year in a hollow tree or leaf nest. Of these not all will be gray, but rather some will be solid black. In southeastern Canada, this is the rule rather than the exception.

EASTERN GRAY SQUIRREL *Sciurus carolinensis*

DECEMBER 30

The male common redpoll, with its rose-stained breast, adds a welcome dash of colour to an often drab winter landscape. An occasional visitor from the arctic or sub-arctic region where it nests, its numbers vary greatly from year to year. Even in a good year you seldom see many of them until after Christmas. A hardy bird, it can survive colder temperatures than any other songbird. At this time of year it gathers in flocks, frequenting forests, fields, orchards and swamps in its search for seeds. Both its song and undulating flight are very similar to those of the goldfinch, with which it often teams up in the winter. Redpolls are very tame and easily approached. Often I can photograph them without having to use a blind.

COMMON REDPOLL *Carduelis flammea*

JANUARY

JANUARY IS A TIME OF BITTER COLD
and deep snow. On especially severe days
there is very little animal life to be seen.
Most creatures lie low in their winter retreats.
But beneath the snow many small rodents
scurry about. Deer yards begin to fill up and
the bucks soon shed their antlers. Although
birds travel less at this time of year, the
occasional arctic species may yet be seen.
Nature is never still.

WHITE-TAILED DEER *Odocoileus virginianus*

Winter can be a difficult time for the white-tailed deer. Deep snow and lack of food can take their toll. Usually solitary, these handsome deer band

JANUARY 2

together into small groups in early December. Their reddish-brown summer coat is replaced by a thicker, coarser gray one that insulates them well enough so that they can sleep comfortably in the snow without melting it. As the snow deepens they are forced to move to traditional 'deer yards' where thick stands of conifers offer some protection from the weather. Here they make a network of well-packed trails that conserve energy and provide a way through the snow should they need a quick escape. Their hooves are too narrow to be of much use for pawing through the snow, so they are forced to survive by browsing on twigs, buds, saplings and evergreen needles. A typical band will inhabit an area of about 120 hectares or 300 acres, or less, depending on the availability of food.

COMMON GOLDENEYE *Bucephala clangula*

JANUARY 6

Although most common goldeneyes migrate south, a few of them winter here on the open rivers. They are also often to be seen along the shore of Lake Ontario. These hardy birds are hesitant to leave their breeding grounds until the freeze-up, at which time they will only travel as far south as need be to find open water. They are powerful fliers, and the whistling sound of their wings as they pass overhead has earned them a nickname, 'the whistler'.

FEMALE GOLDENEYE *Bucephala clangula*

The goldeneye is an expert diver and feeds mainly on molluscs in the winter. It is very timid and so is not often seen up close. The male common goldeneye is black and white, with an iridescent greenish-purple head and a distinctive round white cheek-patch. The female is mainly ash gray with a narrow white collar and a brown head. Both sexes have the characteristic golden-coloured eye.

Although it does not hibernate, the red squirrel remains in its den through very harsh weather. All winter long it spends little time in the trees, but instead it travels an extensive tunnel system that it builds beneath the snow. Though it is an animal of the day, it may on occasion venture out at night. At this time of year the red squirrel grows large ear-tufts and sheds the obvious black stripe down its sides. It feeds mainly on seeds, fungi, cones and nuts. These cones are stored in a large pile known as a midden, which can measure as much as 9 metres or 30 feet across and one metre deep.

JANUARY 11

RED SQUIRREL *Tamiasciurus hudsonicus*

AMERICAN ROBIN *Turdus migratorius*

JANUARY *16*   The first time I saw a robin in the dead of winter I said to myself, 'That poor bird doesn't stand a chance.' I was wrong, and each year more and more of these familiar birds are abandoning their traditional flight to the south and remaining in the north, even in extreme climates. Most people think the robin eats mainly worms and insects, but actually a large part of its diet consists of fruit and berries. Therefore shrubs like mountain ash and various other decorative plantings make it possible for the robin to survive the long winter. The majority of them still winter in the warm Gulf states all the same, and their return in early spring is still a sign to most of us that better weather is on the way.

The American robin gets its name from the fact that it reminded early English colonists of the popular robin or redbreast back home. In actual fact the American robin is not a robin at all. It is a thrush.

The hairy woodpecker (overleaf) is much more shy and less often seen than its smaller look-a-like, the downy. The female lacks the red head- **J ANUARY** 31

patch of the male. A year-round resident of deciduous forests, this bird sleeps in tree holes during the coldest weather. Insects provide three-quarters of its diet. It extracts them from inside wood and under bark on a tree by tapping and listening to see if it has disturbed any insects inside. Both sexes drum on the trees, and not only during the breeding season. The astonishing speed and force of their hammering are possible only because heavy-duty shock-absorbent bones in the head protect the brain and extra-strong neck muscles keep the birds from hurting themselves. While propping itself up against a tree trunk the hairy woodpecker leans back on its stiff tail and braces itself as it hammers. Unlike most birds its has two back toes instead of just one and these give it added support. Also helpful are the bristle-like feathers which cover the nostrils and so protect them from wood dust.

HAIRY WOODPECKER *Picoides villosus*

F E B R U A R Y

FEBRUARY IS SHORT,

but it is cold and stormy, though not as

dark and gloomy as the other winter months.

Many animals now begin searching for mates,

and the groundhog interrupts its winter sleep

early in the month to look for his shadow,

or so the story goes. Numerous wintering birds

gather and roost together into flocks, while some

very hardy species start heading north.

Bitter Nightshade *Solanum dulcamara*

FEBRUARY 5

Originally from Europe, and a relative of both the potato and the tomato, bitter nightshade is a thornless, climbing vine of up to two and a half metres or eight feet long. The crimson berries of this plant are poisonous to most animals but some birds, among them the ruffed grouse, pheasant and black duck, seem to be immune to the poison, which is solanine. The leaves are also toxic and the plant is often called 'deadly night-shade . The toxin has been known to kill cattle, and is certainly not something to feed the children on a picnic. It is a late bloomer, often both flowers and berries occur at the same time, and after the leaves die the berries cling to the vine well into the winter. You may find them anywhere whether in thickets or in clearings throughout North America.

FEBRUARY 6

During the winter, the male goldfinch (overleaf) loses its bright coloration and becomes very difficult to distinguish from the duller female. Goldfinch move in small flocks and often join together with other small finches such as the redpoll and pine siskin. They feed on the catkins of birch and alder, as well as the seeds of various cone-bearing trees. Often you see them hopping on the ground searching for fallen seeds. When in flight these little birds will sing, even at speeds of up to 56 kilometres or 35 miles per hour.

AMERICAN GOLDFINCH   *Spinis tristis*

FEBRUARY 15

The mute swan, which had been semi-domesticated in western Europe for over a thousand years, is now an inhabitant of Ontario and is on the increase. There is usually no mass migration in the fall, and each year more and more of these hardy birds choose to winter along the shores of Lake Ontario. Despite its name it can make sounds similar to a pup's bark and will hiss when disturbed. While nesting the mute swan is very territorial and may attack anyone who gets too close. Swans are well insulated against the cold, and may have as many as 25,000 feathers. Mute swans rarely dive underwater, but they may tip to reach the aquatic plants that make up the bulk of their diet.

MUTE SWAN *Cygnus olor*

FEBRUARY *22*

The sun had just set when a series of loud shrieks echoed across the lake where I was sitting. At first I thought it was a woman screaming for help but there were no roads back there and as far as I knew I was alone. What I heard was the mating call of the Canada lynx, probably the same one that had left its footprints near my place that week. During its mating season in late winter, the usually silent lynx becomes quite vocal. Males yell at each other and at the females as well. A creature of the deep forest, it is very shy and rarely seen. It wears its own snowshoes, a thick growth of hair on the feet which allows it to walk through the deep snow without sinking in too much. I once tracked a lynx well into the bush on my own pair of snowshoes and foolishly followed its tracks along an ice-covered river. Being very light on its feet the lynx had not even left a crack, but I went crashing through down into the freezing water. Struggling to get out of the river I tried to climb the bank but soon I found myself neck-deep in snow. After backing up again I reached down into the water and took off my slush-filled snowshoes. No longer weighed down, I was then able to get back onto the ice and safely to the shore. After taking a few quick shots of the river I headed home, a long hour away. Luckily it was a fairly fine day, and I made it back in good time to dry myself out.

The solitary Canada lynx is active all year round and its thick coat protects it from the coldest weather. The distinctive black ear-tufts are believed to magnify sounds that are muffled by the snowy woods. Although it can weigh up to 18 kilos or 40 pounds, the lynx rarely reaches more than 13 1/2 kilos or 30 pounds weight. Mainly nocturnal, the lynx may begin hunting in late afternoon when it is hungry. During the day the lynx takes shelter under a fallen log or rock ledge. An expert climber, it sometimes rests in trees, and will pounce down upon any unsuspecting animal that happens to pass by. Its most usual prey is the snowshoe hare, and it may eat as many as 200 of them in a fat year. However, it also feeds on other small mammals and birds as well as carrion and has even been known to bring down winter-weary deer. Large kills are cached and covered with snow. The home range is usually up to 2000 hectares or eight square miles though it may travel as far as 100 kilometres or 60 miles in search of food.

CANADA LYNX *Lynx canadensis*

CANADA GOOSE *Branta canadensis*

F EBRUARY *20*

When I was young, to see a Canada goose in winter was a rare delight. Nowadays many of them have abandoned their traditional migratory habits and are either wintering in open-water areas of the Great Lakes or in sanctuaries that offer peace and plenty. These hardy birds are prospering and have more than doubled their numbers since the 1950's. As early as late February the first spring migrants may begin arriving from the south.

WOOD DUCK *Aix sponsa*

Undoubtedly our most beautiful duck, this species is found only in North America. Its Latin name 'sponsa', means 'betrothed' or **F**EBRUARY 27 'promised one' referring to its showy plumage as though it were 'arrayed to be wed'. While it usually spends the winter in the southern states, a few winter around Lake Erie and Lake Ontario. Those which have migrated arrive on their northern breeding grounds in early spring. A bird of the forests, it nests in hollow tree cavities as high as 15 metres or 50 feet off the ground. The female wood duck is not as colourful as her mate. She has a smaller crest, and a distinctive white ring around her eye. While about 90 per cent of the wood duck's diet consists of aquatic plants, it sometimes ventures deep into the woods in search of nuts and berries.

MARCH

MARCH IS A MONTH OF CONTRASTS.
It can be both wintry and springlike. Hibernators
wake up and the first migrants from the south
begin arriving. By the time of the vernal equinox,
when the day and night are of equal length,
the first wildflowers of the year begin poking
up through the soil. The sap flows in the trees and
their buds swell. In shallow ponds and marshes
the ice retreats, freeing the season's earliest
amphibians. There are even insects out and
about if you know where to look.

Mourning Cloak *Nymphalis antiopa*

On warm March days I make a point of searching the woods hoping to see my first mourning cloak of the season. Some years I find them on the wing

MARCH 7

while there is still a fair amount of snow on the ground. This is the best time of the year to get a close look at one, since they are rather sluggish after their long winter sleep, and spend a great deal of time soaking up what little sunshine and warmth there is.

These hardy butterflies spend the winter hibernating in tree hollows or under bark, logs or stones. Stiff and inactive during the bitter cold, they can revive very quickly once the temperature rises. Mourning cloaks are easily alarmed and when approached take off with an audible clicking sound. They get their name from the fact that their wings resemble the dark funeral shawls that were worn by widows in Victorian times.

RED-WINGED BLACKBIRD *Agelaius phoeniceus*

MARCH 9   I never really believe that spring is on its way until the first red-wings arrive from the south. The male's 'kon-ker-ee' is music to my ears after a long, cold winter. Usually the marshes are still icebound when the males start claiming territory as their own. Their bright red epaulets are a badge of maturity and are puffed out to threaten any rival. Once the females arrive, usually a week or two later, the red-wings pair up and begin nesting. The nest is built by the female, who strips off strands of cat-tail to be used in its construction. On average four eggs are laid and incubated by the female alone. Her mate stands guard over their property, driving away any unwelcome intruders.

It's a wonder how a chick manages to escape from its hard-shelled egg. By hatching time there is not much room left inside. However there is a little air pocket at the wide end of the egg into which the chick pushes its beak, using the pocket as a temporary air supply. A day or two from hatch day it can be heard chirping inside. The struggle to break free begins once the chick pecks a hole in the end of the egg with a special egg-tooth on the tip of its bill. It now breathes the fresh outside air for the first time and takes

RED-WINGED BLACKBIRD Chick hatching out

a much-needed rest. Next it turns in its shell and chips a circular groove all the way around. Using powerful muscles on the back of its neck it pushes with all its strength until the shell breaks in two. Totally exhausted it rests once more, awaiting now the first meal from its mother.

 ARCH *15* As soon as the snow begins to melt you can expect to see the killdeer, a member of the plover family. Their repetitious kill-DEEE call is one of my favourite sounds of March. Killdeers often return to the same 300 to 400 square metres or 350 to 475 square yards of territory year after year to raise their young. Their nest is a simple hollow on the ground, often in a totally exposed area. But just try to find it! In all the years I have searched for them I have only found one, and that was quite by accident. Not only do the parents and their eggs blend in perfectly with their surroundings but so do the young. While the adults try to lure you away with their famous broken-wing routine the chicks stay perfectly still, hugging the ground. I nearly stepped on this one before I spotted it.

K ILLDEER *Charadrius vociferus*

Young killdeer

M ARCH 28

Looking a lot like a small dandelion, the coltsfoot is not native to this land but was brought over from Europe by settlers who considered it a cure for coughs. An early spring bloomer, it is found in wasteplaces and along eroded banks. It grows up to 45 centimetres or eighteen inches tall, however most of those I have seen are rather small. Coltsfoot gets its name from its leaves which were thought to resemble a colt's foot. Who says botanists don't have any imagination? If you look underneath these leaves you will notice they are white and hairy.

M ARCH 29

Many people believe the chipmunk is still in a deep sleep during March but actually by mid-month some may have already resumed full activity. In fact, from February onward the male chipmunk regularly leaves his winter den, searching for a female. During the spring, and the autumn as well, chipmunks often call back and forth to each other. Sometimes you can hear a whole community of them chattering in a voice which has been likened to a 'pond full of tenor frogs'.

Eastern Chipmunk *Tamias striatus*

Chipmunks are one of my favourite animals. I love watching them stuff their cheeks full of seeds, as if they must get every last one in their mouths before someone else does. Just how much can they pack away? One determined chipmunk managed to get in seven large acorns while another jammed in an impressive 32 beechnuts.

MARCH *31* A true harbinger of spring, the exquisite spring beauty (opposite) blooms in moist woodlands and along riverbanks often as early as late March. Standing up to 30 centimetres or twelve inches high, its candy-striped flowers close at night or on cloudy, dark days. Spring beauty grows from an underground tuber which was used as food by the Indians and early settlers. I'm told it tastes a bit like a sweet chestnut but I'd rather leave it alone to bloom another year than taste it for myself.

Spring Beauty *Claytonia virginica*

Great are the works of the Lord;
    They are studied by all who delight in them.

PSALM 111:2

ABOUT THE PHOTOGRAPHY

I have been interested in photography since I was a child and made my first 8mm wildlife film at the age of ten. However, it has only been in the last seven years that I have pursued nature photography as a full-time occupation. I use both 2 1/4 and 35 mm systems, though for my wildlife work the smaller format is preferred. I use a limited range of lenses; rarely do I shoot with anything greater than a 300 mm telephoto. Over 95 per cent of all my photographs are taken with manual cameras and I have yet to use an auto-focus lens. Although I own automatic equipment, I am still more comfortable setting everything myself. For the most part I use medium-speed film, therefore few shots are taken without a tripod.

Most of my work is done in the morning or evening. Not only is wildlife more active then, but the lighting is at its best. Although I prefer to use only natural light, sometimes a flash is a necessity, especially when photographing animals in the den, or birds on the nest. Whenever possible, a creature should be photographed unawares or any rate undisturbed in its natural habitat. Only in this way can we hope to achieve an authentic portrait of nature. So it is that I spend the majority of my time seeking out my subjects and getting as close to them as possible. Good nature photographs can rarely be obtained without a lot of prior planning. I could almost count on my fingers the number of times I have stumbled upon a worthwhile picture but I will admit that it does happen on occasion. Simply passing through an area, hoping to see and photograph wildlife there, usually won't result in much. I spend a great deal more time locating and observing animals than I spend actually filming them. I seldom take multiple pictures of the same subject. I used to do so, but now I am very selective. I do not believe that by making scores of exposures you are bound to end up with at least a few good images. You may just end up with nothing but a lot of expense.

If the lighting is bad, if there's no highlight in the eye, or if the background is distracting, I may snap one or two pictures to document the subject but that will be all. Each year I take fewer and fewer photographs, but I still have to work at it all the time and I have to wait and be patient. Even when everything is going well, I still prefer to wait for that one good shot.

SELECTED REFERENCE LIST

Angell, Madeline. *A Field Guide to Berries and Berrylike Fruits*.
Indianapolis: Bobbs-Merrill, 1981

Behler, John L., and Wayne King. *The Audubon Society Field Guide to North American Reptiles and Amphibians*. New York: Alfred A. Knopf Inc., 1979

Bull, John and John Farrand Jr. *The Audubon Society Field Guide to North American Birds (Eastern Region)*. New York: Alfred A. Knopf Inc., 1977

Burt, William Henry. *The Peterson Field Guide Series: A Field Guide to the Mammals of America North of Mexico*. Boston: Houghton Miffin Co., 1976

Calahane, Victor H. *Mammals of North America*.
New York: Macmillan Pub. Co. Inc., 1958

Collins, Henry H. Jr., and Ned R. Boyajian. *Familiar Garden Birds of America*.
New York: Harper & Row Pub., 1965

Conant, Roger. *A Field Guide to Reptiles and Amphibians of Eastern North America*.
Boston: Houghton Miffin Co., 1958

Ferguson, Mary, and Richard Saunders. *Canadian Wildlfowers*.
Toronto: Van Nostrand Reinhold Ltd., 1976

Ferguson, Mary, and Richard Saunders. *Canadian Wildflowers Through the Seasons*.
Toronto: Key Porter Books, 1989

Forsyth, Adrian. *Mammals of the Canadian Wild*.
Camden East: Camden House Publishing Ltd., 1985

Garber, Steven. *The Urban Naturalist*. New York: John Wiley & Sons Inc., 1987

Klimas, John E. and James A. Cunningham. *Wildflowers of Eastern America*.
New York: Alfred A. Knopf, 1974

Lawrence, Ronald D. *The Natural History of Canada*. Toronto: Key Porter Books, 1988

Macdonald, David W. *The Encyclopedia of Mammals*. New York: Facts on File, 1984

Miller, Orson K., Jr. *Mushrooms of North America*. New York: E.P. Dutton and Co., Inc. 1979

Milne, Lorus Johnson. *The Audubon Society Field Guide to North American Insects And Spiders*.
New York: Random House, 1980

Niering, William J. and Nancy C. Olmstead. *The Audubon Society Guide to North American Wildflowers (Eastern Region)*. New York: Alfred A. Knopf Inc., 1979

Peterson, Roger Tory. *A Field Guide to the Birds (Eastern Region)*.
Boston: Houghton Miffin Co., 1978

Pile, Robert Michael. *The Audubon Society Field Guide to North American Butterflies*.
New York: Alfred A. Knopf Inc., 1981

Rehwinkel, Alfred M. *The Wonders of Creation*. Minneapolis: Bethany House Publishers, 1974

Savage, Candace. *The Wonder of Canadian Birds*.
Saskatoon: Western Producer Prairie Books, 1985

Stanek, V.J. *The Illustrated Encyclopedia of Butterflies and Moths*.
London: Octopus Books Ltd., 1977

Terres, John K. *The Audubon Society Encyclopedia of North American Birds*.
New York: Alfred A. Knopf, 1987

Theberge, John B. *Legacy: The Natural History of Ontario*.
Toronto: McClelland & Stewart Inc., 1989

Whitaker, John O., Jr. *The Audubon Society Field Guide to North American Mammals*.
New York: Alfred A. Knopf Inc., 1980

Williams, John G. and Andrew E. *Field Guide to Orchids of North America*.
New York: Universe Books , 1983

Wood, Gerald L. *Animal Facts and Feats: a Guinness Record of the Animal Kingdom*.
Garden City N.Y.: Doubleday, 1972

INDEX OF PLATES

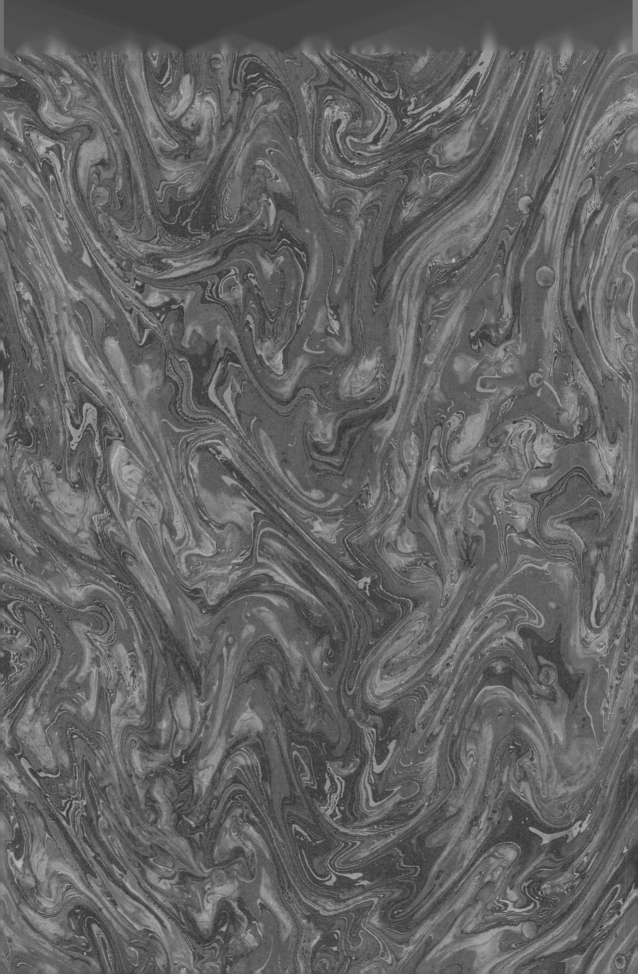